Quick-and-Easy Learning Centers
Phonics

By Mary Beth Spann

SCHOLASTIC PROFESSIONAL BOOKS
New York • Toronto • London • Sydney • Auckland

Dedication

To Terry Cooper and Joan Novelli, with thanks for your friendship, your expert editorial talents, your enthusiasm and warmth. I'm lucky to be learning so much from you both.

Acknowledgments

Much gratitude to my friend and colleague Valerie Williams, first-grade teacher at the E.M. Baker School in Great Neck, New York, especially for her contributions to the "What's in a Name?" center. Thanks also to gifted educator Eileen Griffin, director of curriculum studies for the Griffin Center for Human Development in Guilford, Connecticut, who taught me almost all I know about kid watching.

Copyright © 1996 by Scholastic Inc.
Design by Lauren Leon
Editor: Joan Novelli
Cover illustrator: Rick Brown
Interior illustrator: James Hale

ISBN: 0-590-93094-x

Printed in U.S.A.
12 11 10 9 8 7 6 5 4 3   7/9

Table of Contents

P honics instruction, when presented as an integral component of a language arts program, can offer children important skills and strategies for developing reading and writing abilities. When students are invited to use inquiry methods to investigate and examine meaningful print—that is, print matter that has relevance to their lives—they naturally discover patterns and features involving letter recognition, spelling, letter placement, sound/symbol relationships, letter clusters, and word families that are present in authentic reading situations. As acclaimed educator and author Regie Routman states in her groundbreaking book *Invitations: Changing as Teachers and Learners K–12* (Heinemann, 1991), "Rather than telling students what the sounds and letters are…an inquiry method that has the children 'discover' the sounds and rules works best for engaging students in meaningful phonetic associations."

The phonics activities in this book are designed to enrich your existing language arts curriculum in this way—combining phonics instruction with real-life connections, such as recipes, mail, signs, songs, shopping, and more. Each of the eight learning center plans is designed to reflect students' interests, experiences, and abilities. Center openers suggest ideas for pulling together inviting center environments, and follow with step-by-step directions for making and presenting phonics-related games, activities, and exercises.

The centers are presented in no particular order; flip through and find the ones you like the best and want to try first. Keep in mind that, even though each activity is labeled with its own Phonics Focus, you should feel free to experiment with mixing and matching activities and skills.

Using Learning Centers in Your Classroom

Teaching with learning centers is an exciting process to welcome into your classroom. Like any other process-based methodology, the learning center approach involves change, growth, and experimentation to see what works best for you and your students.

Most of the learning center activities in this book are open-ended and encourage student interaction. Even those activities that focus on learning specific skills, such as letter recognition or spelling, are presented in a playful way so students will gravitate to them again and again. Other benefits of learning centers follow.

- Learning centers offer scheduling flexibility; children can work at centers independently, in pairs, or in small groups.
- Cooperative, open-ended activities allow children to contribute to an outcome or build a knowledge base together rather than competing with one another for the right answer.
- Learning centers wean children away from teacher direction and help them look to themselves and peers for feedback.
- Learning centers encourage choice within a context: choice of which center to enter and which activities to try (depending on how you structure your center time and offerings).
- Learning centers invite children to make decisions about how to approach tasks at a center and how to spend their time, thus encouraging their own responsibility in the learning process.

Students aren't the only ones who benefit from a learning center approach. Learning centers can meet your teaching needs, too. Here are just a few of the ways you can put learning centers to work for you.

- Learning centers can enhance and extend whole-group lessons and activities; many of the center activities in this book are introduced with whole-group mini-lessons designed to set the stage for the independent center work.
- Learning centers can augment your schedule and curriculum, allowing children to play and experiment with greater independence.
- Learning centers can support all areas of the curriculum, though you might want to start with a learning center for the curriculum area you are most comfortable teaching.

The Best Ways to Begin

Begin by choosing a center that appeals to you and try setting up just that one. Remember that the center setups described in this book are suggestions only. You can tone them down, jazz them up, or design your own. You may also want to experiment with other center decorations and designs that are right for you and your space.

Once you've decided on the role of learning centers in your classroom, you'll need to tackle particulars such as how to have students rotate smoothly through the centers over the course of a day or week (alone, in groups, and so on). Some suggestions follow.

- Aim for a balance of activities that students choose themselves and you assign. Teacher-directed assignments ensure that students will experience the activities and social interactions they need, while student-guided choices can help encourage children to take responsibility for their own learning.
- Settle on a comfortable number of learning centers. This number may fluctuate depending on any number of factors (your experience level, room size, class makeup, and so on). Some teachers find that a workable solution is to rotate children through five centers—one center per group, per day. More centers than that may be hard to manage and too difficult for children to visit regularly. Ultimately, you'll need to experiment to discover the right number of centers that works for you.

+ Be flexible about how long you expect students to work at each center. Variables include your schedule, the nature of the activities, and children's interests and needs.
+ Avoid frustration by giving yourself realistic management goals. Reserve a bit of time once or twice a week so you can restock—and rethink—your centers. Use this time to eliminate tired-out centers and assemble new centers as the need arises.

Assessment and Evaluation

Remember that kid watching is one of the best learning center assessment and evaluation tools you have. Take time to observe your students as they engage in a center's offerings. Ask yourself:

+ Do children know what is expected of them?
+ Do they seem eager to get involved?
+ Do they stay on task for a reasonable amount of time?
+ Are they able to pick up where they left off last time?
+ What do they seem to like the best?
+ Are some tasks too difficult? Too easy?
+ What do students return to again and again?

Start a kid-watching journal. Use these notes to help you tinker with your centers and schedules until they best fit your needs and those of your students.

Managing Materials

A workable storage system is a must. Try packing center supplies and activities you are not using (or that you are gathering for future use) into clearly labeled boxes, complete with a list of contents taped to the outside of the box. Include a list of any ancillary materials (such as resource books or children's literature). Consider including a snapshot of the center so you can easily recall what it looked like— and so you can document your success!

Resources ✦✦✦✦✦✦✦✦✦✦✦✦✦✦✦✦✦✦✦✦✦✦✦✦

FOR CHILDREN

You can enrich children's learning experiences at each center by sharing books that support the various phonics focuses. Some suggestions follow.

Center 1: What's in a Name?

A My Name Is Alice by Jayne Bayer (Dial, 1984)

Mary Wore Her Red Dress, and Henry Wore His Green Sneakers by Merle Peek (Clarion Books, 1985)

Tikki Tikki Tembo retold by Arlene Mosel (Henry Holt, 1968)

Center 2: A Cook Nook

Cloudy with a Chance of Meatballs by Judy Barrett (Aladdin, 1978)

The Giant Jam Sandwich by John Vernon Lord with verses by Jane Burroway (Houghton Mifflin, 1972)

Pretend Soup and Other Real Recipes: A Cookbook for Preschoolers & Up by Mollie Katzen and Ann Henderson (Tricycle Press, 1994)

Center 3: Signs of the Times

Harriet Reads Signs and More Signs by Betsy & Giulio Maestro (Crown, 1981)

I Read Signs by Tana Hoban (Greenwillow, 1983)

Center 4: Wheels of Phonics

ABC: A Museum of Fine Arts by Florence Cassen Mayers (Abrams, 1986)

I Spy: An Alphabet in Art by Lucy Micklethwait (Greenwillow, 1992)

Center 5: Rhyme Time

Finger Rhymes collected and illustrated by Marc Brown (E.P. Dutton, 1980)

Read Aloud Rhymes for the Very Young selected by Jack Prelutsky (Alfred A. Knopf, 1986)

Sing a Song of Popcorn: Every Child's Book of Poems selected by Beatrice Schenk de Regniers, Eva Moore, Mary Michaels White, and Jan Carr (Scholastic, 1988)

Where the Sidewalk Ends by Shel Silverstein (HarperCollins, 1974)

Center 6: Read-Along Songs

Over in the Meadow by Louise Voce (Candlewick Press, 1994)

Baby Beluga by Raffi (Crown, 1990)

Silly Songs (Publications International, Ltd., 1993)

Center 7: To Market, to Market

Eating the Alphabet: Fruits and Vegetables from A to Z by Lois Ehlert (Harcourt, Brace, Jovanovich, 1989)

On Market Street by Arnold Lobel (Greenwillow, 1981)

Tommy at the Grocery Store by Bill Grossman (HarperCollins, 1989)

Center 8: The Postal Zone

Dear Mr. Blueberry by Simon James (Macmillan, 1991)

The Jolly Postman by Janet and Allan Ahlberg (Little, Brown & Co., 1986)

FOR TEACHERS

Alpha Stories: Learning the Alphabet Through Flannelboard Stories by Mary Beth Spann (First Teacher Press, 1987). A collection of 26 flannelboard stories and story patterns (one story for each letter of the alphabet), presented with follow-up activities for helping children become familiar with alphabet letters and sounds in a storytelling setting.

Building Literacy with Interactive Charts: A Practical Guide for Creating 75 Engaging Charts from Songs, Poems and Fingerplays by Kristin G. Schlosser and Vicki L. Phillips (Scholastic Professional Books, 1992). Designed to help teachers build a print-rich environment through the use of interactive charts. Included, too, are tips for designing original interactive charts.

Games for Reading by Peggy Kaye (Pantheon, 1984). A fun-filled collection of easy-to-construct learning games for helping children practice phonics and other reading and spelling skills. Excellent resource for your parent lending library, since the activities are really aimed at helping parents interact with their children's learning.

Invitations: Changing as Teachers and Learners by Regie Routman (Heinemann, 1991). The definitive guide for bringing meaningful language experiences to schoolchildren. Includes a host of resources and in-depth information regarding meaningful whole-language theory and practice.

Learning Centers: Getting Them Started, Keeping Them Going by Michael F. Opitz (Scholastic Professional Books, 1994). Everything you need to know to get learning centers up and running in your classroom, complete with management tips, sample floor plans and schedules, ready-to-use activities, and more.

Learning Phonics and Spelling in a Whole Language Classroom by Debbie Powell and David Hornesby (Scholastic Professional Books,1993). Classroom-tested strategies, models, and activities for integrating phonics and spelling.

Moving On in Spelling: Strategies and Activities for the Whole Language Classroom by Cheryl Lacey (Scholastic Professional Books, 1994). Everything you need to integrate spelling—from suggestions for setting up your classroom to tips for record-keeping and evaluation.

Phonics that Work! New Strategies for the Reading/Writing Classroom by Janiel Wagstaff (Scholastic, 1993). A guide for incorporating meaningful, effective decoding strategies into the holistic teaching of reading and writing.

Quick and Easy Learning Centers: Word Play by Mary Beth Spann (Scholastic, 1995). Eight complete learning centers for fostering language development.

Spel...Is a Four-Letter Word by Richard J. Gentry (Heinemann, 1987). A handbook for understanding how learning to spell is a developmental process.

Thematic Poems, Songs and Fingerplays: 45 Irresistible Rhymes and Activities to Build Literacy by Meish Goldish (Scholastic Professional Books, 1993). If you need a rhyme to enrich or extend a classroom theme, chances are this book has something for you. In addition to the theme appeal, the language and structure of most of the selections are simple enough for students to interact with easily (on interactive charts, etc.).

CENTER 1
What's in a Name?

Want your students to practice phonics skills in a truly meaningful context? Try highlighting the phonics inherent in their own names!

Setup Suggestions

Materials
- camera and film (optional)
- craft paper
- large, unruled index cards
- small table or desk plus student chairs
- plastic baskets or shoe boxes to hold supplies
- markers; crayons

Steps
1. Take individual photos of children's faces; mount pictures on index cards. As a variation, have children draw pictures of their faces on the index cards.
2. Cover a bulletin board with craft paper. Label the display WHAT'S IN A NAME?
3. Tack children's photos or pictures (labeled with their names) around the edge of the board to create a border.
4. Place a worktable and chairs (and any supplies needed for each activity) in front of the display.

✦✦✦ ACTIVITY 1 ✦✦✦✦✦✦✦✦✦✦✦✦✦✦✦✦✦✦✦✦✦✦✦✦✦✦✦✦✦✦✦✦
Name Sort

Phonics Focus
sorting names according to various phonetic features

Materials
✦ multicolored sentence strips
✦ thumbtacks
✦ brightly colored yarn
✦ stapler

What to Do
1. Choose a phonics criterion for sorting names, such as:
   • beginning sounds
   • number of syllables
   • silent letters
   • double letters

2. Label sets of sentence strips according to the criterion you choose. For example, if you choose number of syllables, your sentence strips might look like this:

These names have one syllable.

These names have two syllables.

These names have three or more syllables.

3. Tack one set of sentence strips to the top of the display.
4. Staple a length of yarn to separate the display into sections.
5. Invite children to staple their name cards onto the appropriate section on the display.

Follow-up

Look together at the bulletin board display. Talk about how you could arrange the name cards so as to see at a glance how many students' names fit each criterion (e.g., in a bar graph arrangement).

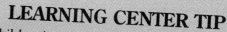

LEARNING CENTER TIP
If some children's names begin with consonant digraphs (two consonant letters that join together to create a new sound [e.g., *sh, th, wh, ch, ph*]), use the yarn to divide the display into thirds and label section 3 with a sentence strip reading: "These names begin with consonant digraphs."

Rearrange the cards and count together the number of names satisfying each criterion, and make labels explaining your findings.

Variations

Try sorting last names, names of family members or pets, or names of characters from favorite stories.

••• ACTIVITY 2 •••••••••••••••••••••••••••••••••••••••
Name Games

Phonics Focus
exploring spelling patterns and rhyming words

Materials
✦ copy paper
✦ activity pages (see pages 14–16)
✦ magnetic alphabet letters (not necessary, but nice) or a supply of alphabet letters printed on 2-by-2-inch pieces of oaktag (place in a box at the center)

What to Do
1. Copy a class set of each Name Games activity page. Place one activity page in the center at a time.
2. Plan a mini-lesson to introduce the first activity page. (See suggested mini-lessons below.)
3. When children complete their activity sheets, schedule sharing time so children can benefit from one another's efforts.
4. Consider displaying finished pages together on a wall to create a "quilt" configuration, or bind pages together in a book and circulate among children's families.

Before asking children to try any of the Name Games activities, use your own name on the chart or chalkboard to model the process. Engage children's help as you "think out loud." For example, when completing the Rhyme Time activity, you might enlist their help to make certain you record as many rhyming words as possible. ("Let's see, my name is Mary, so I'm going to write my name on this first line here. What do you think might happen if I change the first letter of my name? Let's read my new word. How can I make certain that I use as many letters as I can to make new words?"). Demonstrate how to fill in the activity page with your rhyming words. Let children know that their attempts to rhyme may result in real or nonsensical words.

LEARNING CENTER TIP

These activities are bound to produce temporary or invented spellings, that is, spelling approximations that contain many, but not all, of the correctly placed letters. For example, children may suggest that the word *fary* is a real word that rhymes with Mary. View such situations as opportunities to applaud the children's skills ("Wow! You hear correctly that 'fary' rhymes with 'Mary!'"), while moving them on to new understandings and observations. ("But did you know that this word is actually spelled 'ferry,' as in a ferryboat, or 'fairy,' as in a fairy princess? Let's look together at these different spellings.").

⟡⟡⟡ ACTIVITY 3 ⟡⟡⟡⟡⟡⟡⟡⟡⟡⟡⟡⟡⟡⟡⟡⟡⟡⟡⟡⟡⟡⟡⟡⟡⟡⟡⟡⟡⟡⟡⟡⟡⟡
Lift-a-Letter Name Tags

Phonics Focus
+ playing with the alphabet
+ letters and sounds

Materials
+ pastel-colored oaktag (or discarded file folders) cut into 9-by-12-inch pieces (one piece per child)

What to Do

1. Fold the oaktag in half so that you have pieces measuring 4½-by-12 inches.

2. Holding the folded papers horizontally, print each student's name along the bottom edge. Cut between each letter, as shown, just to the folded edge of the paper, to create flaps.

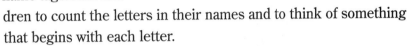

3. Hand out the name tags. Ask children to count the letters in their names and to think of something that begins with each letter.

4. Have children lift each of their flaps and draw or glue pictures beneath each one that represents that letter sound.

5. Display the Lift-a-Letter Name Tags in your hallway or invite children to place them at their desks or cubbies.

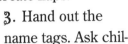

LEARNING CENTER TIP

Using names of friends and family members, make more Lift-a-Letter Name Tags to give as gifts.

CENTER EXTENSIONS ✦✦✦✦✦✦✦✦✦✦✦✦✦✦✦✦✦✦✦✦✦✦

✦ Provide children with rubber alphabet stamps and washable ink pads. Invite them to use the stamps to stamp out responses on their What's in a Name? activity pages (see pages 14–16).

✦ Invite children to bring in alphabet and other word-play games from home. Set aside time for children to explain their games' directions to the group and play.

✦ As a class, compile and learn a collection of songs, rhymes, and chants featuring children's names (for example, the song "Mary Wore a Red Dress" or the jump-rope rhyme "A My Name is Alice"). A good resource for such a collection is *American Children's Folklore,* compiled and edited by Simon J. Bronner (August House, 1988). Consider printing favorites on the pages of a large sketch pad and displaying them in the center for children to read and illustrate.

Name Rhymes

Directions

 1. Write your name on the first line below.
 2. Use the other lines to write words that rhyme with your name.
    They can be silly or real words.

_____

_____

_____

_____

_____

_____

Name Scramble

Directions

1. Write your name on the first line below.
2. From our letter box, pick the letters that spell your name.
3. Move the letters around. See how many other words you can spell using the letters in your name. You may use some or all of the letters to make new words.
4. Copy your new words on the rest of the lines below.

_____

_____

_____

_____

_____

_____

✦✦✦

Name Twisters

Directions

   1. Write your name on the first line.
   2. Think of other words that begin with the first letter in your name.
   3. Write these other words on the rest of the lines below.

_____

_____

_____

_____

_____

_____

✦✦

CENTER 2
A Cook Nook

Cook up a taste of real-life phonics skills with phonics-rich recipes that explore alliteration, spelling variations, homonyms, and compound words.

Setup Suggestions

Materials
+ small table or desk and chairs
+ plastic baskets or shoe boxes to hold supplies
+ two or three paper chef's hats (available at party and paper goods stores)
+ two or three dolls or stuffed animal toys (optional)
+ cookbooks (especially full-color editions and those featuring recipes for children)
+ string or yarn
+ assorted kitchen utensils

Cookbooks for Kids

Children will love *Pretend Soup and Other Real Recipes: A Cookbook for Preschoolers & Up* by Mollie Katzen and Ann Henderson. (See Resources, page 7, for more information.)

Steps
1. If possible, plan to set up your Cook Nook near a bulletin board or blackboard. That way, you can easily display recipes and other charts you and your students design.
2. Display hats on dolls or stuffed animals. Place dolls on the table along with a basket for supplies.
3. Display cookbooks. (A tabletop book rack or any other front-facing bookshelf will be handy.)
4. Use string or yarn to hang kitchen utensils from ceiling wire over the center.

✦✦✦ ACTIVITY 1 ✦✦✦✦✦✦✦✦✦✦✦✦✦✦✦✦✦✦✦✦✦✦✦✦✦✦✦✦✦✦✦
Delicious Alliterations

Phonics Focus
✦ experimenting with alliteration
✦ building alphabet awareness

Materials
✦ reproducible recipe card (see page 21)
✦ magazines with recipes

INTRODUCTORY MINI-LESSON Talk with children about alliteration, the repetition of a sound at the beginning of words. Give some examples that show how alliteration can make language fun (for example, "Peter Piper picked a peck…") and invite children to share some, too. Then look through magazines together for recipes with alliteration in their titles.

What to Do
1. Make 26 copies of the reproducible recipe card.
2. Print one alphabet letter in each of the boxes.
3. Arrange these pages in alphabetical order between construction paper covers; staple along the left-hand side to form a booklet.
4. When children visit the center, invite them to look through magazines and clip recipe titles featuring alliteration.
5. Children can then glue these titles to the corresponding alphabet pages, for example, gluing "Baked Beans" to the B page, "Coconut Custard" to the C page, "Fabulous Fudge" to the F page, and so on.

FOLLOW-UP MINI-LESSON Read the recipe book together, then ask questions such as:
✦ Which alphabet letter page has the most recipe titles on it? Why?
✦ Which alphabet letter page has the least recipe titles on it? Why?
✦ Why do you think people who make up recipes and the writers who write the magazines sometimes use alliteration in recipe titles? (Help children recognize that alliteration can make language bouncy and fun to read.)
✦ Can you brainstorm one more alliterative recipe title I can write on each page of our booklet?

··· ACTIVITY 2 ···
Blend It Up!

Phonics Focus
building awareness of consonant blends

Materials
+ collection of kitchen utensils with names that feature a consonant blend (e.g., *spoon, spatula, whisk, brush, gloves, slotted spoon, fork, plate, grater,* etc.)
+ chart paper

What to Do
1. Cut a piece of chart paper in half horizontally.
2. Invite a child to select a kitchen utensil, place it in the center of a piece of chart paper, then trace around it. Write (or have the child write) the name of the utensil on the drawing.
3. Ask children to think of other words that have the same initial consonant or consonant blend as the utensil. Record these words on the chart paper.
4. Display other utensils and chart paper at the center. Let children trace the utensils and label them, then add words that have the same initial consonants or consonant blends. Display utensil charts so that other students can add words, too.

··· ACTIVITY 3 ···
Interactive Recipe Charts

Phonics Focus
identifying vowel digraphs, homonyms, and compound words

Materials
+ oaktag
+ stick-on notes in assorted colors

What to Do

1. Copy each recipe on page 22 on chart paper or oaktag, and display at the center.

2. Plan three separate mini-lessons to introduce the three phonics features of the recipe titles: vowel digraphs, homophones, and compound words. (See Introductory Mini-Lesson, below.) Begin each mini-lesson by reading through one recipe together. Then take a closer look at the phonics features by having children use different-colored stick-on notes to flag vowel digraphs, homophones, and compound words on each recipe card. (See Introductory Mini-Lessons, below)

3. After the mini-lesson, let children follow up at the center independently or in small groups, flagging more vowel digraphs, homophones, and compound words on the recipe cards. Challenge children to do the same with new recipes you add to the center or that they bring in.

INTRODUCTORY MINI-LESSON

✦ For Recipe 1, Noodle Soup: Use the inquiry method to help children discover the title's separate vowel digraphs *(oo* and *ou)* that each make the same sound. For example, say, "Do you notice anything special about the vowels in *noodle* and *soup?*" Then comb through the rest of the recipe to find other examples of these digraphs. Do they sound the same? Look for examples of other digraphs, too.

✦ For Recipe 2, Flour Flowers: Use the inquiry method to help children notice the title's homophones (words that sound the same, but are spelled differently). Together, find other examples such as <u>knead</u> and <u>dough</u>.

✦ For Recipe 3, Rainbow Popcorn: Use the inquiry method to help children discover that each word in the title is a compound word made up of two smaller words. Find other examples of these compound words in the recipe.

CENTER EXTENSIONS ✦✦✦✦✦✦✦✦✦✦✦✦✦✦✦✦✦✦✦✦✦✦✦

✦ Have children bring in copies of recipes. Examine phonetic features together.

✦ Let children work in pairs, combing cookbooks for vowel digraphs, compound words, and homophones.

✦ Print a recipe in steps on sentence strips. Have children place the strips in proper sequence.

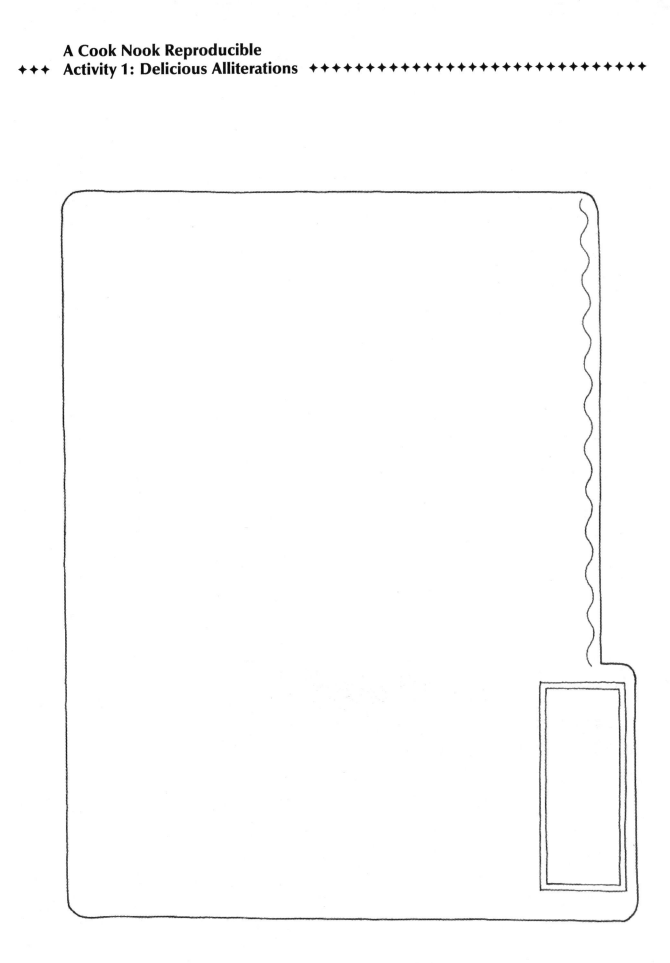

NOODLE SOUP

soup pot
water
one pound egg noodles
colander
one large can vegetable stock
fresh vegetables, cut into chunks
    (tomatoes, carrots, peppers)

1. Bring the soup pot filled with water to a boil. Add noodles, and cook until tender. Strain.
2. Pour soup broth into the pot. Add vegetables. Cook until tender.
3. Add noodles and heat through.

FLOUR FLOWERS

$2/3$ cup vegetable shortening
$3/4$ cup sugar
splash of milk
1 teaspoon vanilla
2 bowls
spoon
2 cups flour
$1\frac{1}{4}$ teaspoons baking powder
$1/4$ teaspoon salt
rolling pin
flower cookie cutters
egg whites and assorted food coloring
clean paintbrushes

1. Mix shortening, sugar, milk, and vanilla in large bowl until well blended.
2. Mix dry ingredients in a separate bowl.
3. Mix together moist and dry ingredients to form dough; chill overnight.
4. Knead the dough to soften it a bit before rolling it out with a rolling pin. Cut into flower shapes with flower cookie cutters.
5. Paint flower cookies with different colors of food coloring mixed with egg whites.
6. Bake on ungreased cookie sheets for about 8 minutes at 350°F.

RAINBOW POPCORN

unpopped colored popcorn (available in supermarkets)
pan with lid (or hot-air popper)
oil
large paper grocery bag
butter and salt (optional)

1. Follow package directions for popping corn.
2. Place popped corn into a large paper grocery bag.
3. Add salt and butter to taste.
4. Fold over the bag top. Shake to mix.
5. Open the bag and eat the rainbow!

CENTER 3
Signs of the Times

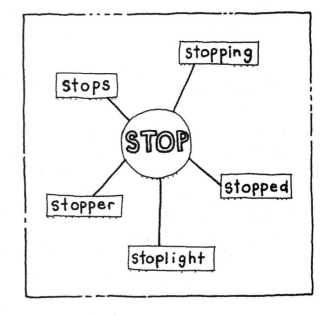

Signs are everywhere—from stop signs to movie marquees—so it makes sense that they're among children's first real-life reading materials. This learning center will show how you can use common signs to help boost students' phonetic awareness in and out of school.

Setup Suggestions

Materials

+ small table or desk and chairs
+ plastic baskets or shoe boxes to hold supplies
+ inexpensive signs, two of each type (OPEN, CLOSED, FOR SALE, and so on; available at office-supply stores)
+ white or light-blue craft paper
+ related children's books, such as:
  The Sign Maker's Assistant by Tedd Arnold (Dial Books for Young Readers, 1992)
  I Read Signs by Tana Hoban (Greenwillow, 1971)

Steps

1. Arrange the supplies and display the books.
2. Cover a bulletin board with craft paper and display one each of the signs around the border. (Save the duplicate signs for Activity 1.)
3. Introduce the center by reading aloud *The Sign Maker's Assistant*. Use the book as a springboard for discussing the importance of signs in our lives.
4. Invite children to look at the signs and comment on any features they notice (colors, sizes, shapes, words, or symbols), and to tell where they may have seen similar (or other) signs.

✦✦✦ ACTIVITY 1 ✦✦✦✦✦✦✦✦✦✦✦✦✦✦✦✦✦✦✦✦✦✦✦✦✦✦✦✦
Sign Collection

Phonics Focus
+ making transitions from temporary to conventional spellings
+ exploring spelling patterns and word endings

Materials
+ shoe box with lid
+ simple signs you've purchased or made (see templates, page 27)
+ scrap paper
+ chart paper

What to Do
1. Cut a slot in the lid and place it on the box.
2. Tape a sign on the outside of the shoe box. (Simple directive-type sign words work best, such as: *go, stop, push, pull, up, down, open,* and *turn.)*
3. Invite children to think of other words that contain the word. For example, if the sign reading STOP is taped to the box, children might write "stops" or "stopped."
4. Have children write the words they think of on scrap paper and place them in the box.
5. During a class meeting, remove the papers from the box and use the new words to create a word web on a piece of chart paper.
6. Examine together the spelling patterns that emerge from these different word versions (e.g., double letters, *-ing* endings). Display the charts for reference.

✦✦✦ ACTIVITY 2 ✦✦✦✦✦✦✦✦✦✦✦✦✦✦✦✦✦✦✦✦✦✦✦✦✦✦✦✦✦
Design-a-Sign

Phonics Focus
copying words

Materials
+ sign shape templates (see page 27)
+ pencils, scissors, markers, crayons, tape, glue, construction paper

What to Do

1. Use a black marker to draw a simple road map on the bulletin board. Include lots of intersections and allow space for glued-on construction-paper vehicles, people, and buildings.

2. Place a class supply of the templates at the center, along with pencils, scissors, markers, crayons, tape, and glue at the center worktable. Talk about signs children see in real life (STOP, WALK, CONSTRUCTION AHEAD, HOUSE FOR SALE, and so on).

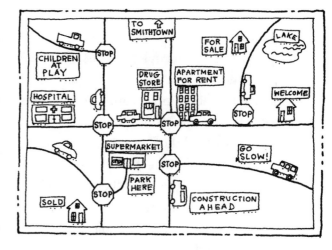

3. Invite children to write simple sign messages on the sign shapes. You might have children write with pencils first, then place an X beneath each letter that is accurately placed, and a check mark beneath each letter that needs revision.

4. Meet with students to review their work and to help them edit their signs for accurate spelling.

5. Invite students to use crayons and markers to decorate their signs, then cut them out and glue to the bulletin board map.

6. Students can also use markers to turn construction paper into buildings, vehicles, trees, people, and so on, and glue these to the mural.

✦✦✦ ACTIVITY 3 ✦✦✦✦✦✦✦✦✦✦✦✦✦✦✦✦✦✦✦✦✦✦✦✦✦✦✦✦✦✦✦✦✦✦✦✦✦✦
Signs of the Times Photo Album

Phonics Focus
building awareness of spelling patterns

Materials
- ✦ camera and film
- ✦ inexpensive photo album with lift-up magnetic pages
- ✦ index cards

What to Do

1. Take your class on a walk in and around your school and neighborhood. Have children take turns using the camera to snap photos of signs they spot. (You may also send the camera home with each child, inviting families to take a predetermined number of snapshots of signs around their homes.)

2. Look at the snapshots together. Have students take turns reading the signs and recounting where each one was located.

3. Make several copies of each photo. Set originals aside.

4. Sort the photocopied versions of the photos and clip each set together with paper clips; place the sets in a plastic basket on the center table.

5. On individual index cards, print a variety of directions asking students to analyze different aspects of the phonetic structure of the signs' words. For example:

- ✦ Find the signs that begin with a consonant (or insert a particular consonant of your choice).
- ✦ Find the signs that begin with a vowel (or insert a particular vowel of your choice).
- ✦ Find the signs that have a short vowel sound (or insert a particular short vowel sound of your choice).
- ✦ Find the signs that have a long vowel sound (or insert a particular long vowel sound of your choice).
- ✦ Find the signs that have a consonant blend (or insert a particular consonant blend of your choice).
- ✦ Find the signs that have a consonant digraph (or insert the digraph of your choice).

6. Place the first phonics criteria card on the first blank page in the album. Demonstrate how to place a sign picture that satisfies the criterion in the photo album.

7. Invite children to visit the center in pairs so they can select copies of the sign pictures that satisfy the phonics criteria card and place them into the photo album.

8. When all the photo cards that satisfy a criteria card have been placed in the album, you can add a new criteria card for children to work on.

CENTER EXTENSIONS ✦✦✦✦✦✦✦✦✦✦✦✦✦✦✦✦✦✦✦✦✦✦

- ✦ Provide stick-on notes so children can create signs for items in the classroom.

- ✦ After reading Tedd Arnold's *The Sign Maker's Assistant,* create silly signs to post all over the school. Print "Just Kidding!" at the bottom of each sign.

- ✦ Share the book *I Read Signs* by Tana Hoban. Invite children to find the same signs in real life.

- ✦ Brainstorm other ways children can use the signs in the classroom. When they are finished with their map mural, they might like to create road and building signs in the block corner.

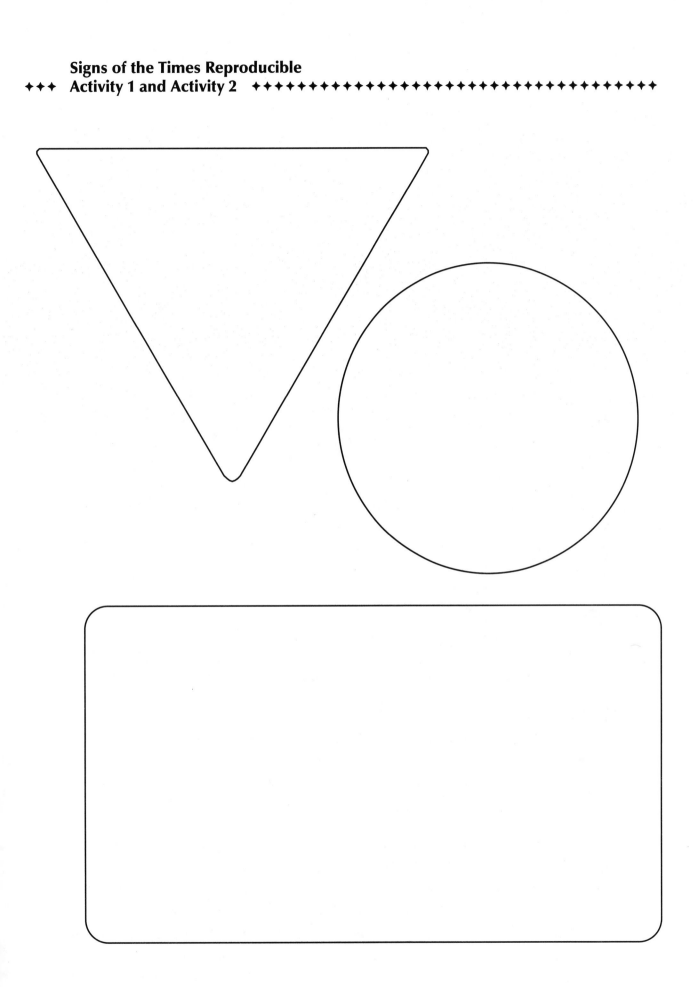

CENTER 4
Wheels of Phonics

Try these circular games for calling children's attention to a host of phonics features. Each game offers lots of variation possibilities—and you're sure to think up lots of your own!

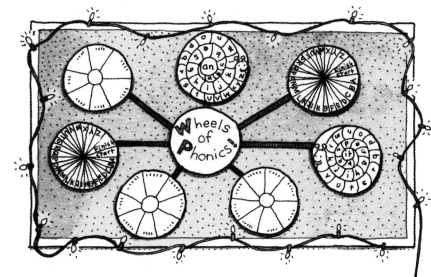

Setup Suggestions

Materials
✦ craft paper
✦ Velcro
✦ at least 7 cardboard circles, approximately 14 inches in diameter
✦ string of holiday twinkle lights long enough to border bulletin board (optional)
✦ glue
✦ glitter
✦ small table or desk plus student chairs
✦ plastic baskets or shoe boxes to hold supplies

Steps
1. Cover a bulletin board with craft paper. In the center of the board staple two lengths of Velcro.
2. Glue the corresponding Velcro strips to the back of one of the cardboard circles so that the circle can adhere to the board.
3. Use glue and glitter to write the words "Wheels of Phonics!" on this circle.
4. Fasten additional Velcro strips to the board and to the rest of the circles to create a display

that resembles a large wheel. (See illustration.) As you introduce the various activities in this center, you can take down the cardboard circles you need, replacing them as children finish.

5. Use the twinkle lights to create a border.

6. Place baskets on tables to hold activity supplies.

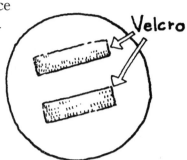

+++ ACTIVITY 1 ++++++++++++++++++++++++++++++++++
Alphabet Wheel

Phonics Focus
practicing alphabet letter sounds and spelling skills

Materials
+ cardboard circle (see Setup Suggestions)
+ ruler
+ markers
+ game playing pieces (anything that will fit on the game spaces)
+ dice
+ magnetic alphabet letters or letter tiles borrowed from other word/letter games

What to Do

1. Use a ruler and marker to divide one of the cardboard circles into 28 segments.

2. Label one of the segments START. Then, moving clockwise from that segment, label each of the rest of the segments with one alphabet letter. Label the final segment FINISH.

3. To play, have children place playing pieces on START. Have the first player roll the dice and move that many spaces clockwise around the circle. Ask the child to name the letter on the space he or she lands on and select that same letter from the magnetic letters (or letter tiles) provided.

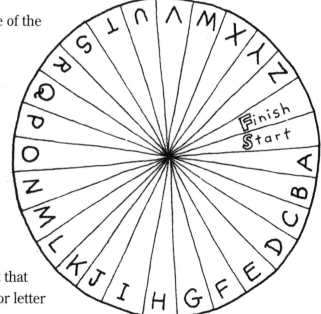

29

4. As children collect letters, they can try to use them to spell words. Remind children to use words they see around the room for possible letter combinations.

5. During a class meeting, remove the papers from the box and use the new words to create a word web on a piece of chart paper.

6. Examine together the spelling patterns that emerge from these different word versions (e.g., letter doubling, *-ing* endings). Display the charts for reference.

Variations

For a cooperative version of this game, children can pool the letters they land on and work together to spell words.

◆◆◆ ACTIVITY 2 ◆◆
Guess My Rule

Phonics Focus
discovering spelling similarities

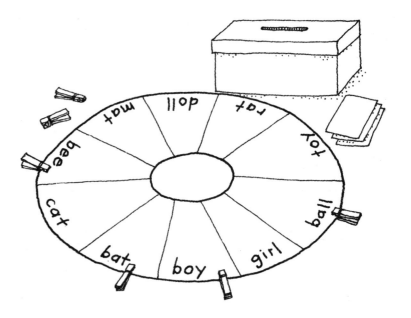

Materials
+ ruler
+ marker
+ cardboard circle (see Setup Suggestions)
+ smaller paper circle
+ glue
+ clothespins
+ covered shoe box (make a slit in the cover)

What to Do

1. Use a ruler and marker to divide one of the cardboard circles into as many segments as you wish. Glue a small paper circle to the center of the wheel and label this circle "Guess My Rule."

2. Decide on a word to place into each segment. You may want to use words from a recognizable source (children's books, thematic vocabulary, children's names, and so on).

3. Decide on a phonics criterion (beginning letter sound, vowel sound, consonant blend, word ending, number of syllables, and so on) that is shared by two or more of the words. Use clothespins to flag these words. (See illustration.)

4. Challenge children to identify what the clothespinned words have in common. Children can record their ideas on small scraps of paper and place the papers into the shoe box.

5. Together, read through students' guesses and then examine the flagged words to see if the guesses are on target.

6. Periodically, move the clothspins to new words to feature a different focus.

Follow-up

Provide blank circles and invite chldren to create their own wheels, using words with which they are familiar. Share students' word wheels at the center.

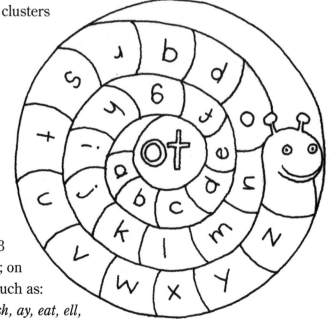

LEARNING CENTER TIP

Make a series of these "Guess My Rule" games featuring different sets of vocabulary words. Children can use the sets to search for features such as:

✦ initial alphabet letters and sounds
✦ vowel sounds
✦ silent letters
✦ consonant blends
✦ consonant digraphs
✦ letter clusters
✦ word endings

✦✦✦ ACTIVITY 3
Snail's Pace

Phonics Focus

blending initial letter sounds with letter clusters (word families) to form words

Materials

✦ old file folders
✦ several large cardboard circles (see Setup Suggestions)
✦ paper fasteners
✦ pencil

What to Do

1. Cut a number of small circles (about 3 inches in diameter) from the file folders; on each one print a common word family, such as:

ack, ail, ain, ake, ale, ame, an, ap, at, ash, ay, eat, ell, est, ice, ide, ill, in, ine, ink, ock, oke, op, ore, ot, ug.

2. Fasten one of the labeled circles to the center of one of the large cardboard circles.

3. Use a pencil to draw a spiral shape on the large circle; end the spiral by drawing the head of a snail.

4. Divide the spiral into segments and print one alphabet letter in each segment. Use a marker to cover pencil marks.

5. Let children take turns blending each initial consonant or consonant blend with the snail's letter cluster to see if they can make a word. Children can keep individual records of words they make or add their words to a collective word chart you set up at the center.

6. Make new game cards featuring different word families. Place them at the center along with the first.

Variation

Print consonant blends on the snail instead of single alphabet letters.

CENTER EXTENSIONS ++++++++++++++++++++++++++

+ Offer children rhyme books so they can look for and record rhyming words in the same family.

+ Provide children with paper circles and have them develop their own game formats. (Books containing word games can help.)

+ Invite children to bring in other word and letter games from home. Set aside time to play!

CENTER 5
Rhyme Time

This center shows how to use poems to explore aural language and spelling variations. Almost any simple, repetitive and/or rhyming poem will do. Children will enjoy bringing in their own favorites to plug into the activities.

Setup Suggestions

Materials

- ✦ brown craft paper
- ✦ overhead projector
- ✦ clock reproducible (see page 37)
- ✦ construction paper (9 by 12 inches) in assorted colors
- ✦ oaktag
- ✦ copy paper
- ✦ children's poetry collections
- ✦ markers
- ✦ strong tape (packing or masking)
- ✦ small table or desk plus student chairs
- ✦ plastic baskets or shoe boxes to hold supplies

Steps

1. Cover a bulletin board with craft paper.
2. Use an overhead projector to enlarge the clock shape on page 37. Project the enlarged shape onto brown craft paper and cut out. The clock must be large enough so that a piece of 9-by-12-inch construction paper fits within the box panel featured on the front of the clock base.
3. Add details to the clock, for example, cutting oval eyes from construction paper. Staple the clock to the bulletin board.
4. Tack a dialogue balloon to the display so the clock appears to be saying "It's Rhyme Time!"
5. Cut out a door shape from oaktag and tape it to the front of the clock base. Use a thumbtack to hold the door closed.
6. Compile a collection of favorite rhyming poems. Make four copies of each poem, then mount originals on construction paper; tack one of them inside the door. Keep the others handy so that you can easily change the poems when you're ready. (See Activity 2.)

✦✦✦ ACTIVITY 1 ✦✦✦✦✦✦✦✦✦✦✦✦✦✦✦✦✦✦✦✦✦✦✦✦✦✦✦✦✦✦✦✦✦✦✦
Line Up

Phonics Focus
✦ identifying rhyming words
✦ building sequencing skills

Materials
✦ copies of favorite poems (see Setup Suggestions)

What to Do

1. Read aloud the poem inside the clock door at the center display. (See Setup Suggestions.) Then place one extra copy of the poem on the worktable, and cut another copy into strips, one line per strip. (Laminate first, if desired.)
2. Have children visit the center to match poem strips to the intact version by placing the strips on top of the complete poem. Talk about the strategies they used to match the strips.
3. For a challenge, close the clock door and remove the worktable copy of the poem. Then have children try to assemble the poem strips in correct sequence.

••• ACTIVITY 2 ••
What's the Same?

Phonics Focus
✦ matching rhyming words
✦ observing spelling patterns

Materials
✦ copy paper
✦ construction paper

What to Do
1. Place a fresh copy of the poem from Activity 1 on the worktable. Cut out the rhyming words from another copy. (Laminate first, if desired.)
2. Challenge children to match the rhyming words to the intact version on the table.

Follow-up
Talk with children about the spelling patterns in the rhyming words. Ask: What do you notice about how the rhyming words are spelled?

••• ACTIVITY 3 ••
World Flags

LEARNING CENTER TIP
Students can store their poems in color-coded folders on the center table, making it easy for you to check their progress and for them to continue working another day.

Phonics Focus
skimming print to locate phonetic features

Materials
✦ highlighting markers
✦ copies of poems, one per child (see Setup Suggestions, step 6)
✦ sentence strips
✦ file folder

After sharing a rhyming poem from your collection with the class, demonstrate how to use different colors of highlighting marker to flag words containing a particular phonic feature. For example, use a yellow highlighter to underline words with short vowels, a pink marker for rhyming words, and a blue marker for words containing blends.

What to Do

1. Place a class set of the selected poem on the worktable.

2. Write directions on sentence strips, showing students which color marker to use for each phonics feature. Have students work on one feature per session. (Leave each sentence strip up even as you add the next one, so students can work on poems at their own pace.)

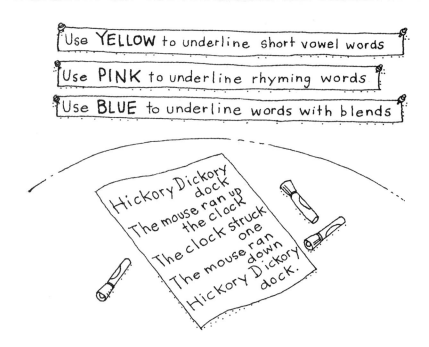

CENTER EXTENSIONS ++++++++++++++++++++++++

+ Print poems on copy paper, leaving plenty of space between each line. Make copies of the poems for students. Invite children to draw pictures above selected words to turn their poems into mini-rebus charts.

+ Print additional copies of the poems, this time omitting key words. For example, for "Five Little Pumpkins Sitting on a Gate," you might omit the word *pumpkin(s)* and ask children to fill in the blanks with new fruit or vegetable words beginning with the letter *p*. Share new versions together.

CENTER 6
Read-Along Songs

This center is similar to Rhyme Time, except that here the meaningful language comes from familiar song lyrics. Begin by visiting the library to locate favorite songs that have been turned into children's books. (See Setup Suggestions.) Then use the activities below to help children sing their way to literacy.

Setup Suggestions

Materials

- ✦ craft paper
- ✦ sheet music
- ✦ tulle netting
- ✦ rubber bands
- ✦ curling ribbon
- ✦ children's books with corresponding music cassettes or CDs
- ✦ one or two music stands
- ✦ small table or desk plus student chairs
- ✦ plastic baskets or shoe boxes to hold supplies
- ✦ cassette player or CD player

Steps

1. Decorate your bulletin board with song sheets.

2. Drape tulle across top of display. At both corners, gather tulle in rubber bands to create "rosettes." Tie curling ribbon around the rosettes to conceal the rubber bands.

3. Place the music stands near the board. Use them to display books featuring illustrated

children's song lyrics, such as *Baby Beluga* by Raffi (Homeland Publishing, 1983) and *Mary Wore Her Red Dress and Henry Wore His Green Sneakers,* adapted by Merle Peek (Clarion Books, 1985).

4. Display additional book titles (along with the tape recorder) on the worktable. Stock the plastic baskets with song cassettes or CDs.

5. Use a length of craft paper to make a banner reading READ-ALONG SONGS. Decorate with a treble clef plus lines resembling a music staff and some musical notes. Curl both ends of the banner so they resemble a scroll. Attach to the top of the display, just under the tulle.

◆◆◆ ACTIVITY 1 ◆◆◆◆◆◆◆◆◆◆◆◆◆◆◆◆◆◆◆◆◆◆◆◆◆◆◆◆◆◆◆◆◆◆◆◆◆◆◆
Songs in Sequence

Phonics Focus
◆ fostering sequencing skills using initial letter cues
◆ building sight word awareness

Materials
◆ chart paper
◆ sentence strips

What to Do
1. Print the lyrics of a favorite song on chart paper and post in the middle of the bulletin board.
2. Sing the song together, underscoring the lyrics as you sing.
3. Print the same lyrics (exactly as they appear on the chart) on sentence strips. (Number the back of the strips so students can self-check the correct sequence.)
4. Invite children to put the lyric strips in order and to check their own attempts.

Follow-up
Talk with children about the strategies they used to help read the strips (for example, initial letters, sight words, and so on).

✦✦✦ ACTIVITY 2 ✦✦✦✦✦✦✦✦✦✦✦✦✦✦✦✦✦✦✦✦✦✦✦✦✦✦✦✦✦✦✦✦
Cloze-ing Song

Phonics Focus
✦ using cloze techniques to draw attention to word endings
✦ identifying rhyming words

Materials
✦ chart paper
✦ stick-on notes
✦ correction fluid

What to Do
1. Print the lyrics of a favorite song on copy paper and on chart paper. Display the chart paper on the bulletin board.
2. Sing the song together using a pointer to underscore the lyrics as you sing.
3. Print the same lyrics (exactly as they appear on the chart) on copy paper.
4. Use stick-on notes to mask selected lyrics on the chart version of the song. For example, you may want to mask rhyming words, any repetitive word, or just word endings.
5. Use correction fluid to mask the same features on the copy-paper version of the song. Draw a blank line space to replace the masked letters or words.
6. Make a class set of the song sheets.
7. Have children fill in the blanks with the words or letters they believe are missing.

✦✦✦ ACTIVITY 3 ✦✦✦✦✦✦✦✦✦✦✦✦✦✦✦✦✦✦✦✦✦✦✦✦✦✦✦✦✦✦✦✦✦✦
Count the Beats

Phonics Focus
practicing syllabification

Materials
✦ chart paper
✦ copy paper
✦ rhythm instruments (such as hand drums or sticks and cans)

Demonstrate how to use rhythm instruments to play and count out the beats in a song. Offer children a chance to do the same.

What to Do

1. Print the lyrics of a favorite song (not the one you used in the mini-lesson) on chart paper and post in the middle of the bulletin board display. Print the same lyrics (exactly as they appear on the chart) on copy paper. Make a class set.

"<u>If</u> <u>you</u>'re hap <u>py</u> and <u>you</u> <u>know</u> <u>it</u>

<u>Cl ap</u> <u>your</u> <u>Hands</u>..."

2. Sing the song together, using a pointer to underscore the lyrics as you sing.

3. Sing the song again, this time inviting children to use rhythm instruments to count out the beats in the song lines.

4. Have children use pencils to draw horizontal lines beneath lyrics on their own song sheets to indicate how the lyrics are broken into syllables.

CENTER EXTENSIONS ++++++++++++++++++++++++++

+ Print lines of song lyrics on separate pieces of paper. Have children illustrate the lines, then bind the papers into books for classmates to read.

+ Provide a variety of songs on tape for children to listen to at the center and songbooks for children to page through.

+ Invite children to substitute new lyrics for familiar songs. Print the different versions on separate pieces of chart paper (using a contrasting color marker to print any new lyrics) and post together for children to read and sing.

CENTER 7
To Market, to Market

Supermarkets are real-life reading labs complete with signs, labels, lists, newspapers, flyers, package print, posters, and magazines. Why not set up shop in your classroom so students can play store while stocking up on all the reading opportunities such a print-rich setting has to offer.

Setup Suggestions

Materials

+ small plastic baskets or shoe boxes
+ empty bookcase or cardboard cubes stacked and glued together
+ plastic play food and clean, empty containers saved from food, soaps, etc. (labels intact)
+ play cash register and play money, or adding machine and tape, or handheld calculator and receipt book
+ tables or desks
+ chart pad and marker
+ discarded magazines, children's activity books, and file-folder holder
+ play shopping cart and/or paper shopping bags

Steps

1. If possible, plan to set up your shopping center near a bulletin board and/or blackboard. That way, you can easily display shopping-related reading materials or handmade store posters you and your students design.

2. Place tables or desks perpendicular to each other to form a checkout area. Put your cash register, adding machine, or calculator in place. Store the paper shopping bags on, in, or beneath the counter.

3. Stock bookcase shelves with the empty containers and the small plastic baskets or shoe boxes. Fill these containers with the play fruits and vegetables.

4. To create a magazine rack, fill the plastic file-folder holder with the magazines and activity books, and place on the checkout counter.

✦✦✦ ACTIVITY 1 ✦✦✦✦✦✦✦✦✦✦✦✦✦✦✦✦✦✦✦✦✦✦✦✦✦✦✦✦✦✦✦✦✦✦✦✦
Memory Match

Phonics Focus
✦ sight word reading
✦ sound/symbol relationships

Materials
✦ mini-boxes saved from individual serving-size boxes of cereals and single-load sizes of laundry detergent
✦ scissors

What to Do
1. Trim the box fronts from at least 5 or 6 pairs of different boxes for a total of 10 or 12 box fronts. (There is no limit to the number of box front pairs you may include in the game; the more you collect, the more challenging the game becomes, and the more mini-box reading children will engage in.)

2. Place box front cards facedown in an array of rows and columns.

3. Let players take turns selecting two cards in an attempt to make a match. As players turn over the cards, encourage them to read aloud any print they recognize.

4. If the cards do not match, the player turns them over. If the cards match, the player keeps the pair and takes another turn. (For a less competitive version, simply have players leave matching pairs faceup in place.)

> **LEARNING CENTER TIP**
> Reserve a set of the same cereal and soap boxes used in your game; place these extras on the store shelves so children can interact with familiar print as they play.

FOLLOW-UP MINI-LESSON After children have had a few chances to play the mini-box memory game, meet with them to take a closer look at the cards. Ask questions such as:
✦ Can you find any of the same words on any of the mini-boxes?
✦ What kind of cereal (or soap) is this? How do you know?
✦ How many words can you find that begin with the letter _____?

✦ How many words can you find that contain the vowel _____?

✦ Can you find any rhyming words?

✦ Which words are used to make us want to buy the cereal (or soap)?

✦✦✦ ACTIVITY 2 ✦✦✦✦✦✦✦✦✦✦✦✦✦✦✦✦✦✦✦✦✦✦✦✦✦✦✦✦✦✦✦✦✦✦✦✦✦
Peek-a-Box

Phonics Focus
✦ letter clusters
✦ initial consonant sounds

Materials
✦ cardboard containers (saved from food, toy, and soap products, and so on)
✦ scissors
✦ light-colored oaktag
✦ stapler
✦ markers

What to Do

1. Prepare the T-scopes. (See T-scope Directions, right.)

2. Show children the box front without the letter strip in place. Read the target word(s) together.

3. Insert the letter strip and move it along so the new letters substitute for the original ones printed on the box.

4. Invite children to read the new words this device helps to create. How many real and silly words can they make?

T-SCOPE DIRECTIONS

1. Cut out the fronts of cardboard containers.

2. Select one or two easy-to-recognize words printed on the box fronts. (Words that are graphically stylized or that spell popular brand names work best.) Cut two slits on either side of the initial consonants.

3. From the oaktag, cut a paper strip approximately 24 inches long and slightly less wide than the two slits you cut in the cardboard.

4. Thread the strip through the slits so that it covers the initial consonant. Move the strip along, printing a series of letters that differ from the ones the strip is concealing.

LEARNING CENTER TIP

Place a supply of box fronts and blank strips in your learning center; demonstrate to children how they can print letters of their choice on the strips, then use the strips to read new words on the boxes.

✦✦✦ ACTIVITY 3 ✦✦✦✦✦✦✦✦✦✦✦✦✦✦✦✦✦✦✦✦✦✦✦✦✦✦✦✦✦✦✦✦✦✦
Coupon Collages

Phonics Focus
+ alphabet awareness
+ sound/symbol relationships

Materials
+ coupons and grocery store sale circulars
+ glue
+ marker
+ children's scissors

LEARNING CENTER TIP

As children complete collages, bind them into a book. Then post new phonics chart challenges for children to complete.

What to Do
1. Fold several pieces of chart paper into fourths. Unfold and trace over the fold lines to divide each paper into four parts. Post these on a bulletin board or wall near your learning center.
2. Decide which phonetic features you want to focus on (initial consonant sounds, blends, digraphs, word ending clusters, and so on). Print one of these on each chart quadrant.
3. Offer children a supply of store coupons and circulars. Invite them to cut out words that contain one or more of the target phonetic features.
4. Have children glue the words directly onto the charts, thus creating a series of phonics collages.

CENTER EXTENSIONS ✦✦✦✦✦✦✦✦✦✦✦✦✦✦✦✦✦✦✦✦✦✦✦✦✦✦✦

+ Have children sort store coupons according to criteria such as color, product type, savings, etc.

+ Provide children with lined paper cut into strips and invite them to make pretend shopping lists, using packages from the center's activities for ideas.

+ Challenge children to find out how many recipes they can find on product packaging. Try making a recipe or two in class.

+ Collect adjectives (or descriptive words) featured on food packages.

CENTER 8
The Postal Zone

This center encourages students to put their phonics skills to work while writing. The activities are designed to create meaningful contexts for students' reading and writing. They also offer you a chance to model writing skills.

Setup Suggestions

Materials
+ craft paper
+ markers; crayons
+ shoe boxes (one per child)
+ construction paper in assorted colors
+ flag template
+ unruled index cards
+ glue
+ small table or desk and chairs
+ plastic baskets or shoe boxes to hold supplies

Steps
1. Decorate the edges of a bulletin board to resemble the perforation marks on a stamp.
2. Hang a paper flag that reads THE POSTAL ZONE on the upper left-hand corner of the display.
3. Have children tape or glue construction paper over their boxes, as shown, then decorate their shoe boxes like mailboxes. They can use the template to make flags for their mailboxes. (Have each child cut two, then glue them back to back. Poke a hole in each box, push the paper fastener through the flag, then the box.) Have children write their names on index cards and glue them to the front of their mailboxes.
4. Line up the mailboxes side by side on shelves near the bulletin board.

✦✦✦ ACTIVITY 1 ✦✦✦✦✦✦✦✦✦✦✦✦✦✦✦✦✦✦✦✦✦✦✦✦✦✦✦✦✦✦✦
Junk Mail Collection

Phonics Focus
matching letters and sight word configurations

Materials
junk mail (fliers, letters, brochures, coupons, envelopes)

What to Do
1. Send home a letter requesting donations of junk mail for your Postal Zone center (the larger the print, the better).
2. Let children share their contributions with the class and post on the center bulletin board.
3. Each day, post a sentence strip asking children to locate a different phonics feature in the mail:
   ✦ Find ten words that have the sound of a short *a* as in *apple*.
   ✦ Find seven words that begin with the letter *t*.
   ✦ Find five words belonging to the *at* family.
4. Children can write and initial their finds on stick-on notes and put on the edge of the display.

> **LEARNING CENTER TIP**
> While children may not be able to read every word on the junk mail, you can help them recognize those words that appear frequently.

✦✦✦ ACTIVITY 2 ✦✦✦✦✦✦✦✦✦✦✦✦✦✦✦✦✦✦✦✦✦✦✦✦✦✦✦✦✦✦✦✦✦✦
Message Center

Phonics Focus
practicing sound/symbol relationships and spelling skills

Materials
notepaper

What to Do
1. Write a note to each child asking for volunteers to become a writing buddy to another child. Deliver the notes to the children's mailboxes, raising the red flags to indicate messages are inside.
2. Pair children with writing buddies; help children to write and revise notes to each other.
3. Help children decipher one another's notes if necessary. Encourage children to continue writing to their buddies and to anyone else they wish.

✦✦✦ ACTIVITY 3 ✦✦✦✦✦✦✦✦✦✦✦✦✦✦✦✦✦✦✦✦✦✦✦✦✦✦✦✦✦✦✦✦✦
Mail-Order Problem Solving

Phonics Focus
+ identifying sound/symbol relationships
+ practicing spelling skills
+ spiral-bound notebooks

Materials
+ puppet

INTRODUCTORY MINI-LESSON Pretend that your puppet friend is always getting into sticky situations and writes to the children for help. (The puppet's dilemmas can mirror those that your students may be struggling with.)

What to Do
1. After introducing your problem-laden puppet to the children, invite the puppet to write his or her feelings in the pages of a journal.

2. Have the puppet leave messages in the journal describing a series of problems (one at a time) and asking for advice.

3. Leave the journal in the Postal Zone center. Invite children to read the messages (with as little assistance from you as possible), and write and sign responses.

4. Occasionally read problems and responses aloud. Share the puppet's reactions as he or she tries the advice.

CENTER EXTENSIONS ✦✦✦✦✦✦✦✦✦✦✦✦✦✦✦✦✦✦✦✦✦✦

+ Invite family members to mail messages to students using the school address. Distribute these in students' mailboxes.

+ Provide each child with a blank postcard (or card stock cut to regulation postcard size). Invite them to decorate, write, and address their postcards. Make a class trip to the post office to mail the cards.

+ Have children take turns bringing the puppet home for visits. Include a journal for children to record their adventures. Share the journal with the class.